Lonely planet KIDS

THE BIG BOOK OF

TRAIN

ACTIVITIES

WRITTEN BY LAURA BAKER
ILLUSTRATED BY SOPHIE FOSTER

CAPITAL CRISSCROSS

PLACE THESE CAPITAL CITIES IN THE GRID.
LOOK CAREFULLY AT THE NUMBER OF LETTERS TO HELP YOU.

5 LETTERS
ABUJA (Nigeria)
PARIS (France)

6 LETTERS
ANKARA (Turkey)
OTTAWA (Canada)

7 LETTERS
BEIJING (China)

8 LETTERS
CANBERRA (Australia)
KINGSTON (Jamaica)

9 LETTERS
BUCHAREST (Romania)

HINT:
START WITH
THE LONGEST
WORD!

Beijing first became China's capital more than 700 years ago.

STEAM TEAM

LOOK CAREFULLY AT THIS PICTURE.
HOW MANY OF EACH ITEM CAN YOU COUNT?

Steam trains were the first type of trains. They burned coal to heat water. The water turned to steam and powered the train.

Write your answers here:

= _____ | = _____   = _____

CITY SLEUTHING

SOME LETTERS FROM THESE MAJOR CITIES HAVE GONE MISSING! CAN YOU FILL IN THE BLANKS USING THE MISSING LETTERS BELOW?

CITIES

1. S Y _ _ E Y

2. I S T _ _ B U L

3. S H A _ _ H A I

4. L O _ _ O N

5. T O R _ _ T O

6. C H I _ _ G O

MISSING LETTERS

CA   DN   ND   AN   ON   NG

WORKING ON THE RAILROAD

HOW MANY WORDS CAN YOU MAKE FROM THE LETTERS IN THE WORD "RAILROAD"? WHAT IS THE LONGEST WORD YOU CAN MAKE?

RAILROAD

Trains that take people to and from work are called commuter trains.

PACK-DOKU

FILL IN THE GRID SO THAT EACH ROW, COLUMN, AND SECTION CONTAINS ALL THE LETTERS OF THE WORD "PACK."

P	A		K
A			
K		A	P

STATION SEARCH

CAN YOU FIND ALL THE WORDS IN THE GRID?

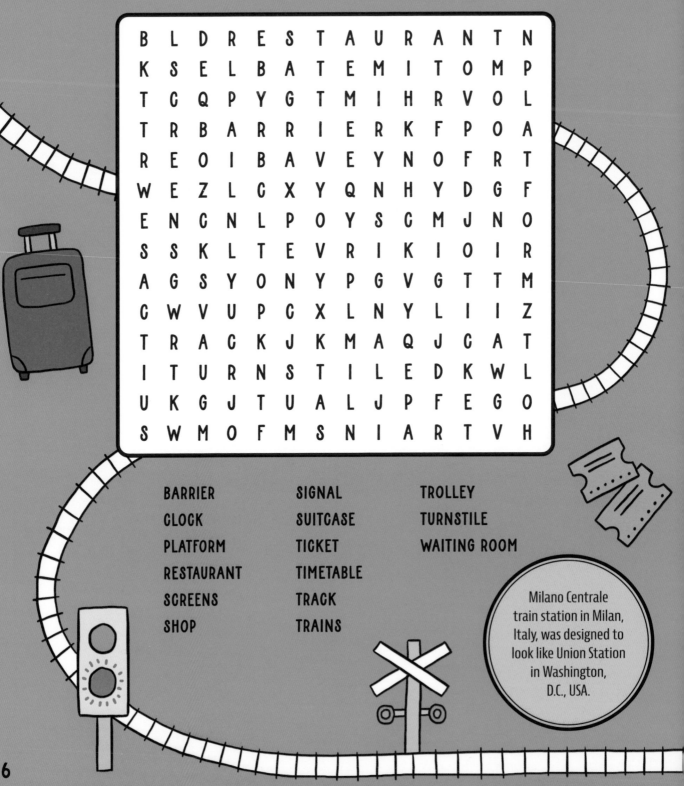

B	L	D	R	E	S	T	A	U	R	A	N	T	N
K	S	E	L	B	A	T	E	M	I	T	O	M	P
T	C	Q	P	Y	G	T	M	I	H	R	V	O	L
T	R	B	A	R	R	I	E	R	K	F	P	O	A
R	E	O	I	B	A	V	E	Y	N	O	F	R	T
W	E	Z	L	C	X	Y	Q	N	H	Y	D	G	F
E	N	C	N	L	P	O	Y	S	C	M	J	N	O
S	S	K	L	T	E	V	R	I	K	I	O	I	R
A	G	S	Y	O	N	Y	P	G	V	G	T	T	M
C	W	V	U	P	C	X	L	N	Y	L	I	I	Z
T	R	A	C	K	J	K	M	A	Q	J	C	A	T
I	T	U	R	N	S	T	I	L	E	D	K	W	L
U	K	G	J	T	U	A	L	J	P	F	E	G	O
S	W	M	O	F	M	S	N	I	A	R	T	V	H

BARRIER

CLOCK

PLATFORM

RESTAURANT

SCREENS

SHOP

SIGNAL

SUITCASE

TICKET

TIMETABLE

TRACK

TRAINS

TROLLEY

TURNSTILE

WAITING ROOM

Milano Centrale train station in Milan, Italy, was designed to look like Union Station in Washington, D.C., USA.

RUNNING LATE

QUICK, HELP THE PASSENGER FIND A CLEAR
PATH TO THE TRAIN! AVOID ALL THE OBSTACLES,
HAZARDS, AND CROWDS OF PEOPLE AS YOU GO.

Japan's trains
are almost never
late. The country has
the timeliest trains
in the world.

START

TO THE PLATFORM ⬇

FINISH

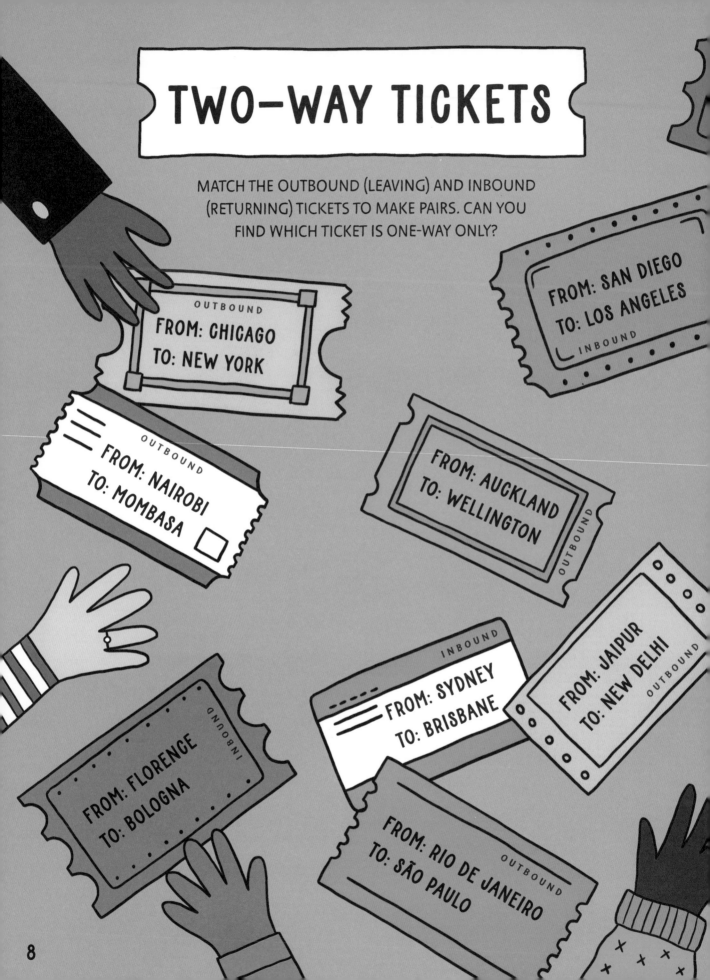

TWO-WAY TICKETS

MATCH THE OUTBOUND (LEAVING) AND INBOUND (RETURNING) TICKETS TO MAKE PAIRS. CAN YOU FIND WHICH TICKET IS ONE-WAY ONLY?

OUTBOUND
FROM: CHICAGO
TO: NEW YORK

FROM: SAN DIEGO
TO: LOS ANGELES
INBOUND

OUTBOUND
FROM: NAIROBI
TO: MOMBASA

FROM: AUCKLAND
TO: WELLINGTON
OUTBOUND

INBOUND
FROM: SYDNEY
TO: BRISBANE

FROM: JAIPUR
TO: NEW DELHI
OUTBOUND

INBOUND
FROM: FLORENCE
TO: BOLOGNA

FROM: RIO DE JANEIRO
TO: SÃO PAULO
OUTBOUND

DESTINATION: ANYWHERE

IF YOU COULD TAKE A TRAIN ANYWHERE IN THE WORLD, WHERE WOULD YOU GO? SKETCH YOUR DREAM DESTINATION HERE.

A TO Z

WHAT KINDS OF THINGS MIGHT YOU SPOT ON A TRAIN JOURNEY? CAN YOU THINK OF A WORD FOR EVERY LETTER OF THE ALPHABET? BE AS CREATIVE AS YOU LIKE!

Animals

B

C

D

E

F

G

H

I

J

K

L

M

N

O

P

Q

R

S

T

U

V

W

X

Y

Z

Different trains run on different types of power sources. Some use fuel like diesel, some use steam, and others use electricity.

Switzerland is home to the longest train tunnel in the world. Running through the Swiss Alps mountain range, it is about as long as 560 soccer fields!

TUNNEL VISION

COLOR IN THIS PICTURE USING THE KEY AT THE BOTTOM OF THE PAGE.

1 = YELLOW   2 = RED   3 = GREEN   4 = PURPLE   5 = BLUE   6 = BLACK

CARRIAGE CODES

SOLVE THE PROBLEMS IN THE CARRIAGES. THEN FILL IN THE GRID AT THE BOTTOM OF THE PAGE BY MATCHING THE NUMBERS TO THE LETTERS IN THE ENGINE WINDOWS. NOT ALL LETTERS ARE USED!

T $12 + 8 =$ ☐

E $22 - 3 =$ ☐

I $16 - 9 =$ ☐

L $4 + 6 =$ ☐

N $3 + 12 =$ ☐

P $15 + 9 =$ ☐

R $13 - 5 =$ ☐

S $11 + 2 =$ ☐

A $12 + 6 =$ ☐

U $18 - 2 =$ ☐

Which country has the longest stretch of straight railway in the world?

18	16	13	20	8	18	10	7	18

The first steam train started running in 1804.

PLATFORM PUZZLE

CAN YOU SPOT ALL THESE ITEMS ON THE BUSY PLATFORM?
CHECK THEM OFF AS YOU GO.

Grand Central Station in New York City has 44 platforms, more than any other train station in the world.

☐ TEDDY

☐ GREEN HAT

☐ POTTED PLANT

☐ DOG COLLAR

☐ UMBRELLA

☐ ORANGE BOW

SLEEPING BABY

GUITAR

WATCH

SEVEN PIGEONS

WALKING STICK

BLUE TIE

SUDOKU CHOO-CHOO

FILL IN THE GRID SO THAT EACH ROW, COLUMN, AND SECTION CONTAINS ALL THE LETTERS OF THE WORD "RAIL."

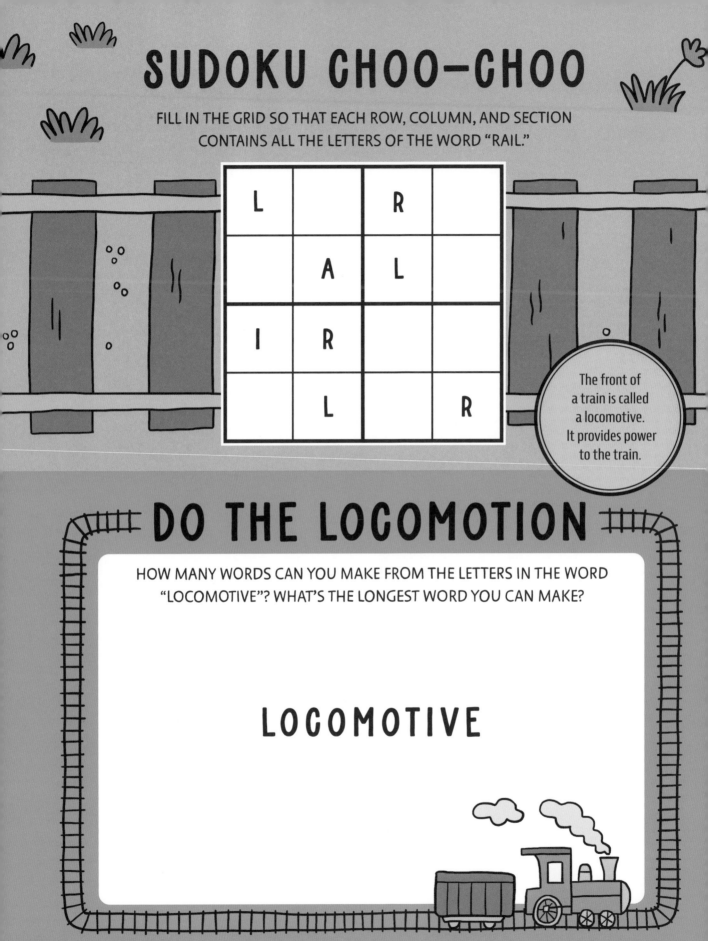

L		R	
	A	L	
I	R		
	L		R

The front of a train is called a locomotive. It provides power to the train.

DO THE LOCOMOTION

HOW MANY WORDS CAN YOU MAKE FROM THE LETTERS IN THE WORD "LOCOMOTIVE"? WHAT'S THE LONGEST WORD YOU CAN MAKE?

LOCOMOTIVE

TRAIN TO CATCH

WHICH PASSENGER ARRIVES AT THE STATION IN TIME TO CATCH THE NEXT TRAIN?

NEXT TRAIN 10:30

MAY MISSIT

DIJA KATCHITT

DON BELAYTE

A train car's wheels have a rim that fits onto the tracks to keep the wheels in place.

MONEY, MONEY, MONEY

LOOK AT THESE CURRENCIES FROM AROUND THE WORLD.
CAN YOU FIT ALL THE WORDS IN THE GRID?

3 LETTERS
YEN

4 LETTERS
EURO
RAND
REAL

5 LETTERS
FRANC
POUND
RUPEE

6 LETTERS
DOLLAR

Some of the earliest types of currencies were seashells and beads. They were traded for goods.

MAKING CONNECTIONS

SOLVE THE CLUES AND FILL IN THE CROSSWORD.

ACROSS

2. A passage that allows trains to go under water or through hills
4. The place where cars or people stop to let trains pass
6. The machine that powers a train
7. A fuel used for the first trains
8. The rails that a train follows
9. A fast train that makes very few stops

Before railroads were invented, horses pulled carriages on "wagonways." These were like wooden railroads.

DOWN

1. The place where trains stop to drop off and pick up passengers
3. The paper or electronic proof needed to board a train
5. A cover for passengers waiting for the train outside

ON THE BOARD

LOOK CLOSELY AT THE ARRIVALS AND DEPARTURES BOARDS SHOWING TRAINS LEAVING AND ARRIVING FROM DIFFERENT CITIES IN EUROPE. THEN ANSWER THE QUESTIONS BELOW.

ARRIVALS

Time	From	Platform	Expected
09:30	DUBLIN	2	ON TIME
09:46	BERN	1	09:50
09:55	LYON	7	ON TIME
10:05	HAMBURG	5A	CANCELLED
10:11	NICE	3	10:09
10:20	GENEVA	8	ON TIME
10:30	PRAGUE	4	11:30

2
One train is arriving to and then departing from the same platform five minutes later. What is its final destination?

_____

3
A passenger is arriving from Bern and wants to catch the train to Berlin. Will they make it?

_____

4
Which train arrived early?

_____

1
Which train is the most delayed?

_____

20

The Paris to Moscow Express is one of the longest direct train journeys in Europe. It takes more than 36 hours.

DEPARTURES

Time	Destination	Platform	Expected
09:35	PARIS	2	ON TIME
09:36	BRUSSELS	5B	ON TIME
09:45	LONDON	3	09:54
10:00	BERLIN	1	ON TIME
10:02	RENNES	4	CANCELLED
10:10	FRANKFURT	7	10:28
10:15	BIRMINGHAM	2	ON TIME

5
I want to go to Brussels. Which platform should I go to?

_____

6
Someone arrived at the station at 09:40 to catch a train to Paris. Did they make it?

_____

7
Which platform has the most trains coming and going?

_____

8
How many minutes late is the train going to Frankfurt?

_____

TRAIN JUMBLE

UNSCRAMBLE THESE WORDS TO DISCOVER DIFFERENT TYPES OF TRAINS. USE THE CLUES TO HELP YOU.

At first, people were afraid to ride passenger trains. They were worried the train's speed would make it hard to breathe.

1. A train that uses a track made of just one rail or beam: **OORMAINL** _ _ _ _ _ _ _ _

2. A train that only makes a few stops so it can get to its destination quickly: **PSERXSE** _ _ _ _ _ _ _

3. A train powered by magnets that hovers above the track: **LGMAEV** _ _ _ _ _ _

4. A train that travels on tracks on city roads: **MRAT** _ _ _ _

5. A train that carries cargo instead of people: **GHRIEFT** _ _ _ _ _ _ _

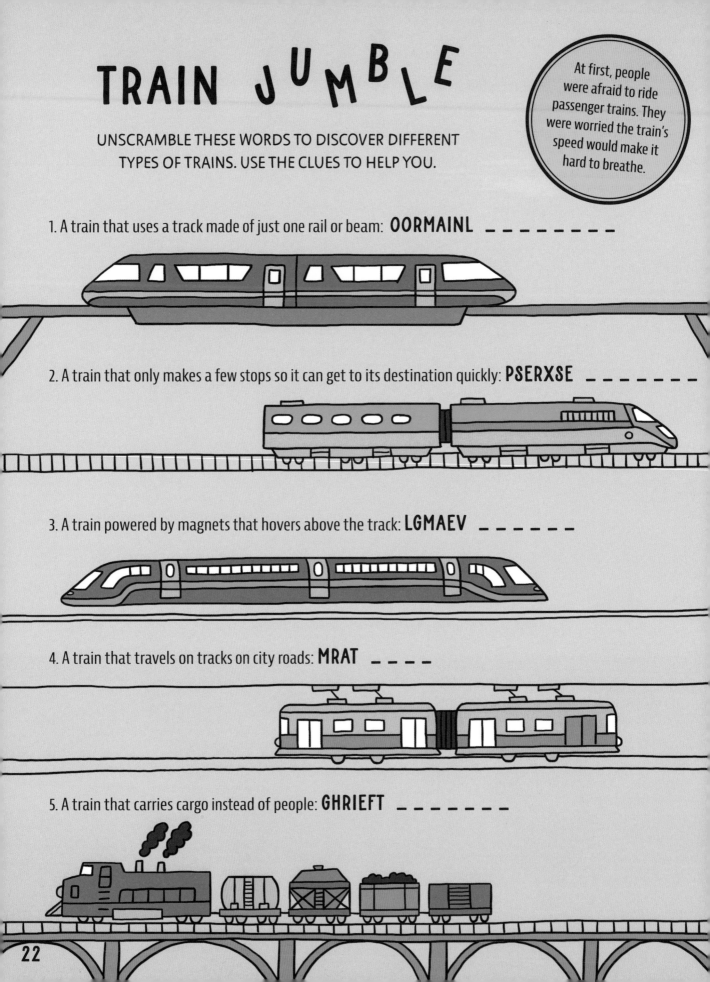

ALL ABOARD!

WHO IS BLOWING THE WHISTLE AT THE STATION?
CONNECT THE DOTS TO FIND OUT, THEN COLOR THE PICTURE.

When steam trains were first invented, the train whistle was called a "steam trumpet."

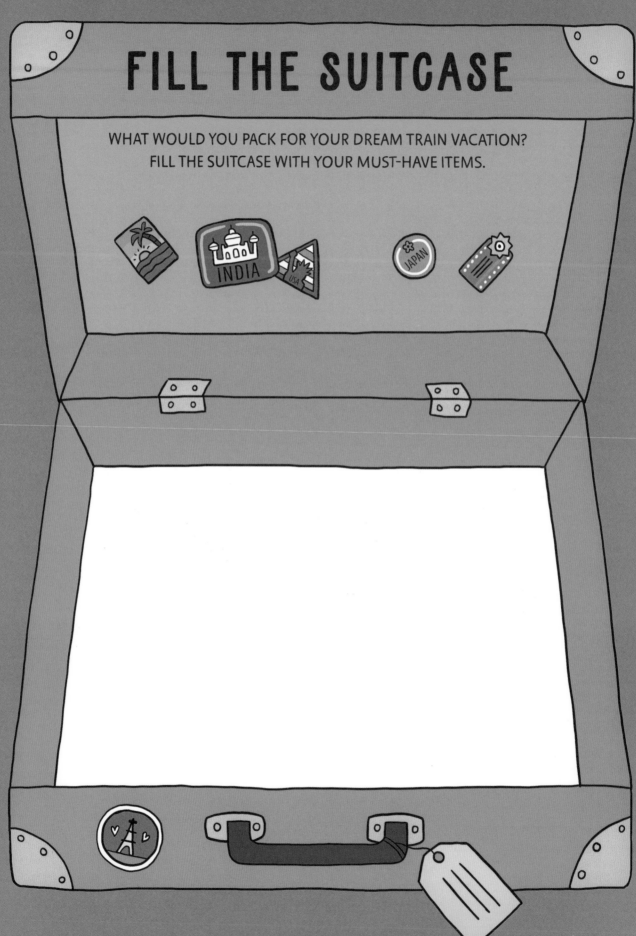

FILL THE SUITCASE

WHAT WOULD YOU PACK FOR YOUR DREAM TRAIN VACATION?
FILL THE SUITCASE WITH YOUR MUST-HAVE ITEMS.

UP THE MOUNTAIN

HELP THIS CLIMBER FIND HER WAY UP THE PATH TO THE TRAIN STATION AT THE TOP OF THE MOUNTAIN.

The Qinghai-Tibet Railway is the highest in the world. Trains roll past glaciers and snow-capped mountain peaks.

FINISH

START

25

THROUGH THE WINDOW

LOOK AT THAT VIEW! FIND AND
CIRCLE 10 DIFFERENCES BETWEEN
THESE TWO PICTURES.

POSTCARD PUZZLE

UNCOVER THE HIDDEN MESSAGE BY CRACKING THE CODE.

The first postcards had no pictures. Decorating postcards and collecting them became a popular hobby in the early 1900s.

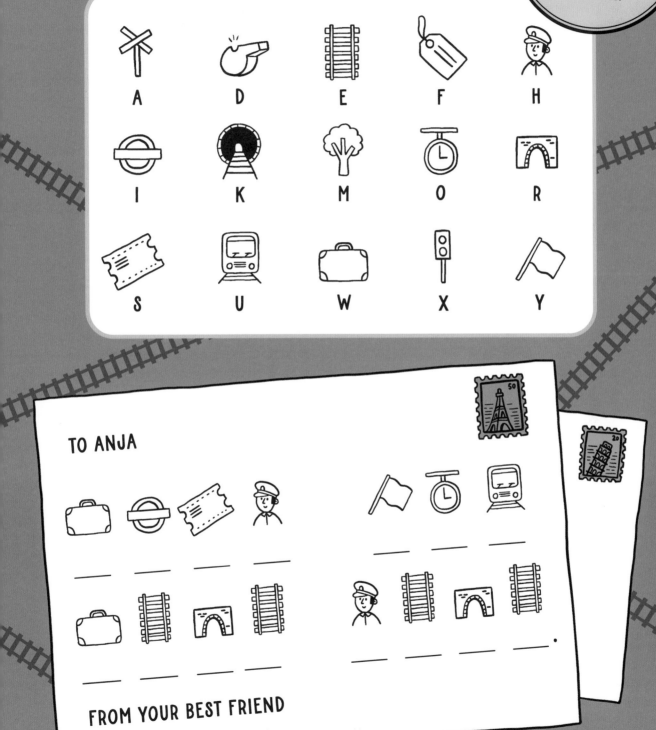

PACKING UP

IT'S TIME TO PACK UP! THESE ARE SOME IMPORTANT ITEMS NEEDED FOR A TERRIFIC TRIP. CAN YOU FIT THEM ALL IN THE GRID?

Before suitcases were commonly used, travelers would keep their belongings in large, heavy trunks.

9 LETTERS
HAIRBRUSH

5 LETTERS
BOOKS
SOCKS

6 LETTERS
TICKET
SNACKS
PILLOW

7 LETTERS
CLOTHES
PAJAMAS

10 LETTERS
HEADPHONES
TOOTHBRUSH
TOOTHPASTE

THE LAUGH TRACK

DRAW LINES TO MATCH EACH
JOKE TO ITS PUNCHLINE.

A freight train carries goods such as food, coal, wood, and many other items that people use.

1. What do you call a late steam train?

2. Why are train drivers so good at being sneaky?

3. What do you call a train with a cold?

4. Why couldn't the elephant ride the train?

5. When does a dog go at the exact same speed as a train?

A. There was no room for her trunk!

B. When it's a passenger!

C. They are great at covering their tracks!

D. Achoo-choo train!

E. A slow-comotive!

WAIT AND SEE

CAN YOU SPOT THESE ITEMS IN THE WAITING ROOM?
CHECK THEM OFF AS YOU GO.

- [ ] NEWSPAPER
- [ ] SANDWICH
- [ ] GUITAR CASE
- [ ] BASEBALL CAP
- [ ] CAT CARRIER
- [ ] ICE CREAM

RED NECKLACE

GREEN TOY TRAIN

RAINBOW SUITCASE

CLOCK

COFFEE CUP

PHONE CHARGER

Trains that have bedrooms where people can snooze are called "sleeper trains." They usually carry passengers on long-distance journeys.

NAME GAME

HOW GOOD IS YOUR TRAIN GENERAL KNOWLEDGE? CIRCLE
THE CORRECT ANSWER TO EACH OF THESE QUESTIONS.

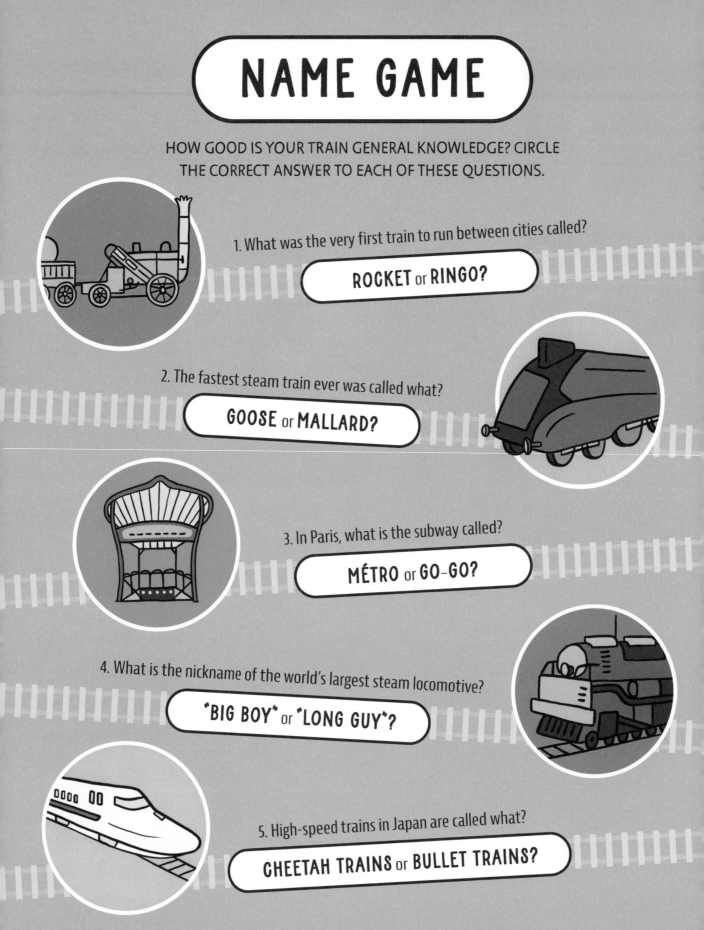

1. What was the very first train to run between cities called?

ROCKET or RINGO?

2. The fastest steam train ever was called what?

GOOSE or MALLARD?

3. In Paris, what is the subway called?

MÉTRO or GO-GO?

4. What is the nickname of the world's largest steam locomotive?

"BIG BOY" or "LONG GUY"?

5. High-speed trains in Japan are called what?

CHEETAH TRAINS or BULLET TRAINS?

CRYPTIC CARRIAGES

TRAIN YOUR BRAIN! CAN YOU FIGURE OUT THESE PERPLEXING PUZZLES?

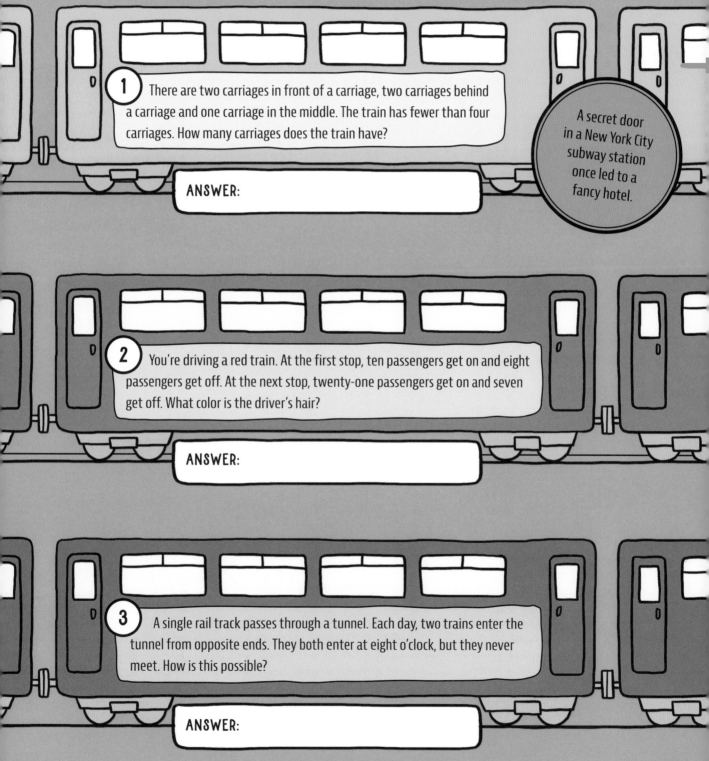

1 There are two carriages in front of a carriage, two carriages behind a carriage and one carriage in the middle. The train has fewer than four carriages. How many carriages does the train have?

ANSWER:

A secret door in a New York City subway station once led to a fancy hotel.

2 You're driving a red train. At the first stop, ten passengers get on and eight passengers get off. At the next stop, twenty-one passengers get on and seven get off. What color is the driver's hair?

ANSWER:

3 A single rail track passes through a tunnel. Each day, two trains enter the tunnel from opposite ends. They both enter at eight o'clock, but they never meet. How is this possible?

ANSWER:

TIC-TRACK-TOE

TAKE TURNS DRAWING AN "X" OR AN "O" IN THE GRIDS. WHO CAN GET THREE IN A ROW FIRST? LINES CAN GO HORIZONTALLY, VERTICALLY OR DIAGONALLY.

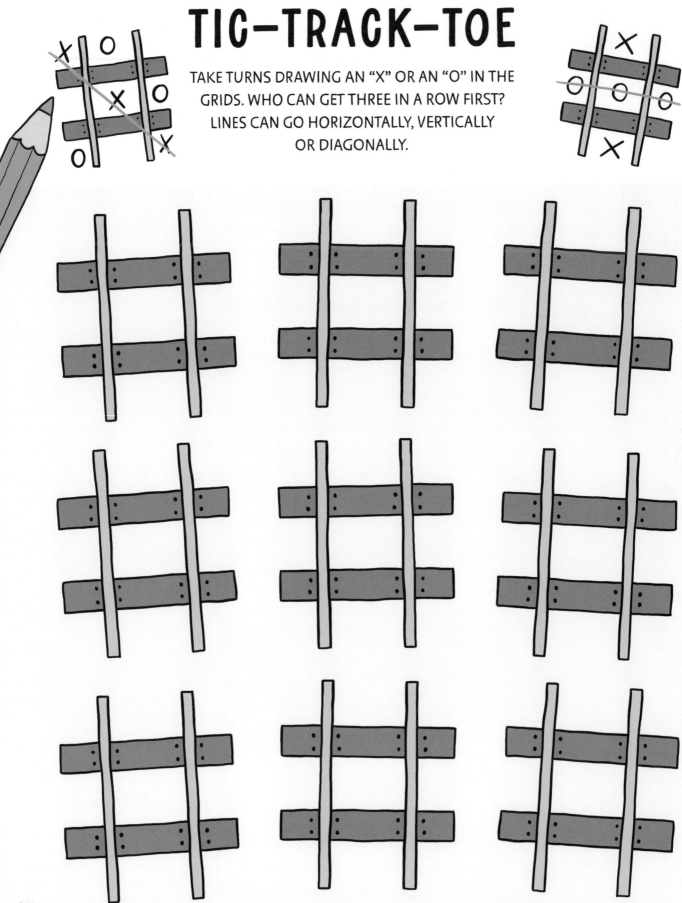

34

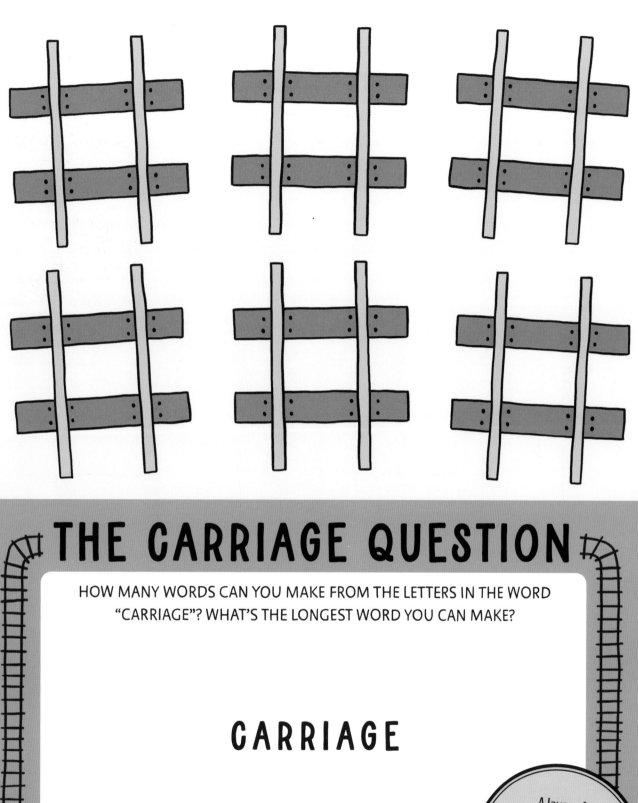

THE CARRIAGE QUESTION

HOW MANY WORDS CAN YOU MAKE FROM THE LETTERS IN THE WORD "CARRIAGE"? WHAT'S THE LONGEST WORD YOU CAN MAKE?

CARRIAGE

A layer of gravel sits underneath railroad tracks, keeping the tracks stable and preventing plants from growing.

DRAWING ON STEAM

FOLLOW THE STEPS TO DRAW YOUR OWN STEAM TRAIN.

1 Draw a large square. Then draw a rectangle on its side, connected to the right side of the square. Draw a line below both boxes for the ground.

2 Draw two large circles connecting the bottom of the square to the line. Then draw three smaller circles on the line, below the rectangle.

3 Draw a triangle to the right of the circles, as shown. Then add a small, long rectangle above the three small circles.

4 Draw two windows in the large square, plus a long rectangle below them. Add a roof to the top of the square.

36

5

At the front of your train, draw a funnel shape above the rectangle to give the train a smokestack. Then draw a bell beside the funnel.

6

Add a small headlamp facing forward, and draw a curved line at the front of the rectangle to round off the train.

7

In the top left of the first large circle, draw a small square. Then draw two horizontal lines to connect this box to the small rectangle above the wheels.

8

Draw spokes on all five wheels, plus extra details to make your train look more interesting. Then add some smoke coming out of the smokestack.

9

Color your train and add a name to the plaque below the windows. Choo choo!

WILD RIDE

IMAGINE YOU ARE ON AN AFRICAN TRAIN SAFARI.
DRAW THE ANIMALS YOU CAN SEE OUT THE WINDOW.

RIDING ALONG

CAN YOU FIND ALL THE WORDS IN THE GRID?

```
H D C O N D U C T O R K R E
C I M W H Q E G A G G U L S
V P N H P C X Y E C B L O N
R Z A Q D R I V E R D M R T
L F T S X G T C Y I Z R A R
R A C K S K Y V N K M E I A
T X G Q V E R I N U S L B Y
O L U T N R N Z S I B O D F
I S E D V G W G B I C H O N
L K L T C N R M E J G P O U
E Q M A Y B C N K R C N R L
T F R B H Y I U N W R U S I
V T N L P O M W I N D O W L
Q Z F E A B R H E N M C R X
```

CONDUCTOR   RACK

DINING CAR   SEAT

DOOR   SIGNS

DRIVER   TABLE

EXIT   TOILET

LUGGAGE   TRAY

PASSENGER   WINDOW

GOING UNDERGROUND

LOOK CLOSELY AT THIS PICTURE OF A SUBWAY CAR. WHAT
DO YOU SEE? TRY TO REMEMBER AS MUCH AS YOU CAN,
THEN TURN THE PAGE TO TEST YOUR MEMORY.

GOING UNDERGROUND

London's first underground trains had no windows.

THINK BACK TO THE PICTURE OF THE SUBWAY CAR ON THE PREVIOUS PAGE. CAN YOU ANSWER ALL OF THE QUESTIONS BELOW?

1
What color was the dog's collar?

_____

2
What did the sign on the wall say?

_____

3
What did the man with a mustache have in his hand?

_____

4
How many people were wearing glasses?

_____

5
What color was the balloon?

_____

6
How many people were in the subway car?

_____

CROSSING BRIDGES

COLOR IN THIS PICTURE USING THE KEY BELOW. ADD SOME PASSENGERS TO THE TRAIN WINDOWS TOO.

The world's tallest railroad bridge is 359 m (1,180 feet) above India's Chenab River. It is almost 30 m (100 feet) taller than the Eiffel Tower!

1 = GREEN   2 = BLUE   3 = RED   4 = GREY   5 = YELLOW

FIELDS OF FUN

FIND A FRIEND OR FAMILY MEMBER AND
PLAY THIS GAME TOGETHER.

Using a pen or pencil, take turns connecting two side-by-side dots horizontally or vertically (not diagonally). When you complete a full square, write your initial in the box and take another turn.

As you play, think about how you can keep your opponent from making squares. When the entire grid is full of completed squares, count your initialed boxes.

The person with the most completed squares wins!

POETRY IN MOTION

WRITE AN ACROSTIC POEM ABOUT TRAINS. USE THE LETTERS OF THE WORD "TRAIN" TO START EACH LINE.

T _____

R _____

A _____

I _____

N _____

In the Netherlands, all trains are powered by energy from the wind. Wind energy is clean, meaning it does not pollute the air.

WHAT DOES THE SIGN SAY? USE THE CODE
TO UNCOVER THE MESSAGE.

A	C	E	F	G	H	I	K	L	M	N	O	R	S	T	U	W	Y

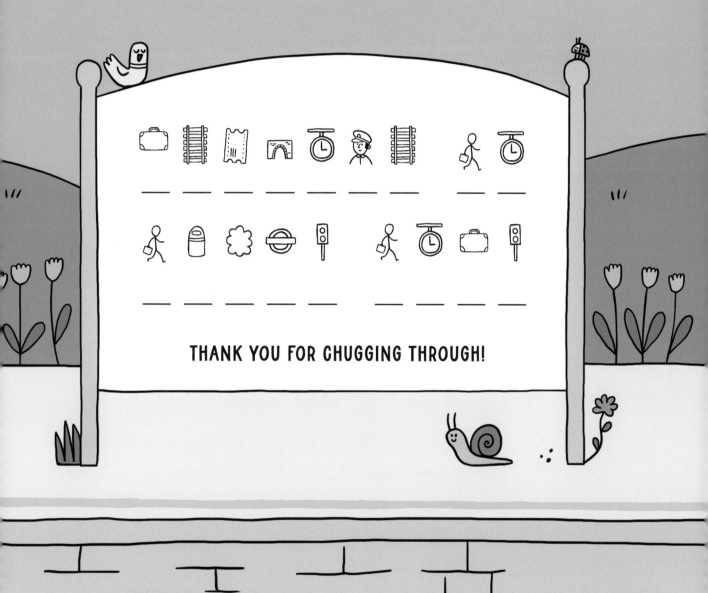

W E L C O M E   T O

T R A I N   T O W N

THANK YOU FOR CHUGGING THROUGH!

TRAIN ART

DESIGN A NEW LOOK FOR THIS TRAIN.
WHAT COLORS AND PATTERNS WILL YOU USE?

COMING THROUGH!

CONNECT THE DOTS TO DISCOVER WHAT IS TRAVELING THROUGH THIS BUSY CITY. COLOR THE PICTURE WHEN YOU'RE DONE.

A tram is a type of electric train. It runs on tracks and gets its power from electrical cables that run above it.

THE HISTORY MYSTERY

LOOK AT THIS LIST OF PEOPLE WHO PLAYED A PART IN THE HISTORY OF TRAIN TRAVEL. CAN YOU FIT THE WORDS IN BOLD CAPITALS INTO THE GRID?

5 LETTERS
EMILE Bachelet:
One of the first inventors of the maglev train

HIDEO Shima:
A designer of Japan's first bullet train

6 LETTERS
John **FOWLER**:
Designer of the world's first underground railroad system

WERNER von Siemens:
One of the inventors of the world's first electric railroad train

7 LETTERS
George **PULLMAN**:
Inventor of the luxury sleeping car

10 LETTERS
George **STEPHENSON**:
Inventor of the first fast trains to travel between cities

Richard **TREVITHICK**:
Inventor of the 1804 steam locomotive

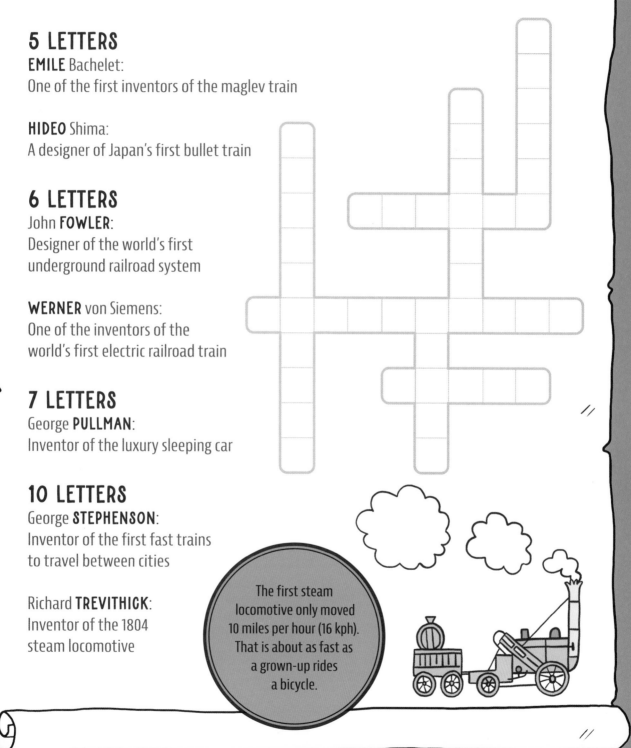

The first steam locomotive only moved 10 miles per hour (16 kph). That is about as fast as a grown-up rides a bicycle.

COUNTLESS COUNTRIES

CAN YOU THINK OF A COUNTRY FOR EVERY LETTER
OF THE ALPHABET? FILL THEM IN HERE.

Argentina

B

C

D

E

F

G

H

I

J

K

L

M

N

O

P

Q

R

S

T

U

V

W

X

Y

Z

There are 195 countries in the world. Africa is home to 54 of them, making it the continent with the most countries.

NAME THAT PART

UNSCRAMBLE THESE WORDS TO DISCOVER DIFFERENT TRAIN PARTS. USE THE CLUES TO HELP YOU.

1. These help the train stop:

KSREBA

_____

2. Where the train operator sits and controls the train:

BGA

_____

3. The round parts that move the train on the track:

SHLEEW

_____

4. The place for passengers to go in and out:

ODRO

_____

5. The large window at the front of a train that the driver uses to see ahead:

ESDLWIDNHI

_____

6. The parts of a train that light the way ahead:

TDSGELIAHH

_____

A ballast cleaner is a machine used to clean the gravel (or ballast) that makes up the track bed.

END OF THE LINE

UNSCRAMBLE THESE WORDS TO REVEAL A VARIETY OF DESTINATIONS. USE THE CLUES TO HELP YOU.

A sunny place with sand and sea

1 AHCEB

_____

A large town

2 TICY

_____

A building containing interesting historical and scientific things

3 UMMUES

_____

A place where children go to play

4 LUDNYRAPOG

_____

A high, snowy hill

5 NUNMATIO

_____

A quiet, rural area outside the city

6 TCIYUONERSD

_____

A ruined or grand building, often with turrets

7 LAESCT

_____

A place to see a play or musical

8 ERTTEHA

_____

TRAIN TRIVIA

SOLVE THE CLUES AND FILL IN THE CROSSWORD.

ACROSS

2. In New York City, the underground train is called the _ _ _ _ _ _
5. A steam _ _ _ _ _ _ _ _ _ _ is powered by burning a fuel such as coal
7. In 19th-century America, this material was often used as fuel for trains instead of coal
8. The type of power used by many modern city railroads
9. This Asian country was the first to introduce high-speed bullet trains

Horse-drawn stagecoaches were used to carry people before trains existed. The first stagecoaches were used in London around 1640.

DOWN

1. Large country "down under" with the first solar-powered train
3. The UK's capital city, and the first in the world to have an underground railroad
4. Before trains, people made long journeys in _ _ _ _ _ -drawn stagecoaches
6. The Orient Express was a long-distance train that traveled between Istanbul in Turkey and this famous French city

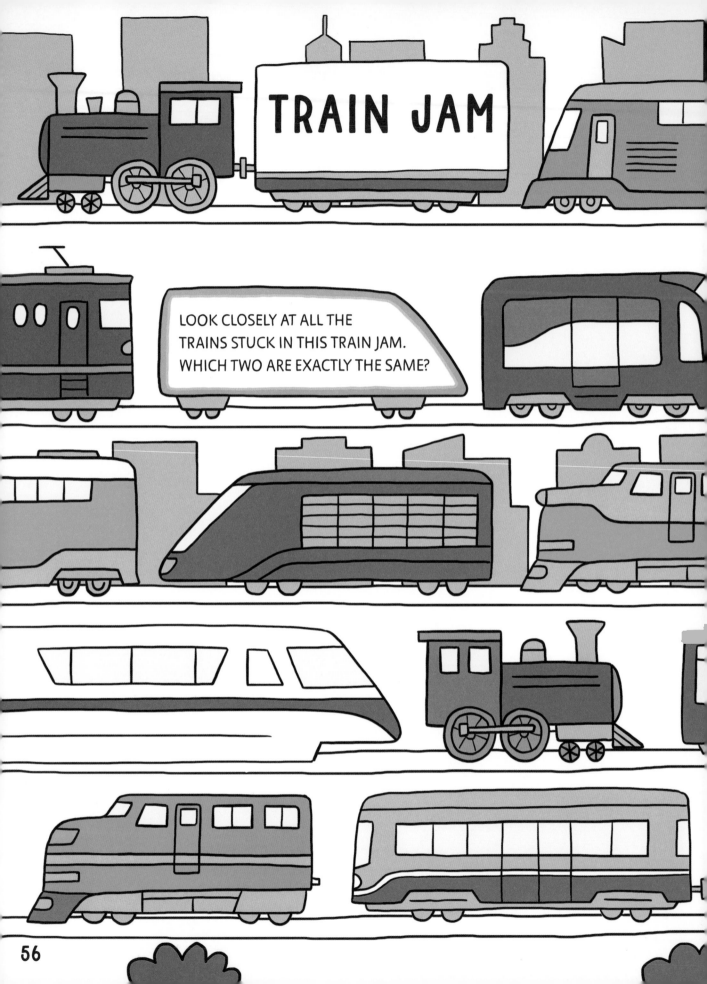

TRAIN JAM

LOOK CLOSELY AT ALL THE TRAINS STUCK IN THIS TRAIN JAM. WHICH TWO ARE EXACTLY THE SAME?

SEARCHING FOR TRAINS

CAN YOU FIND ALL THE WORDS IN THE GRID?

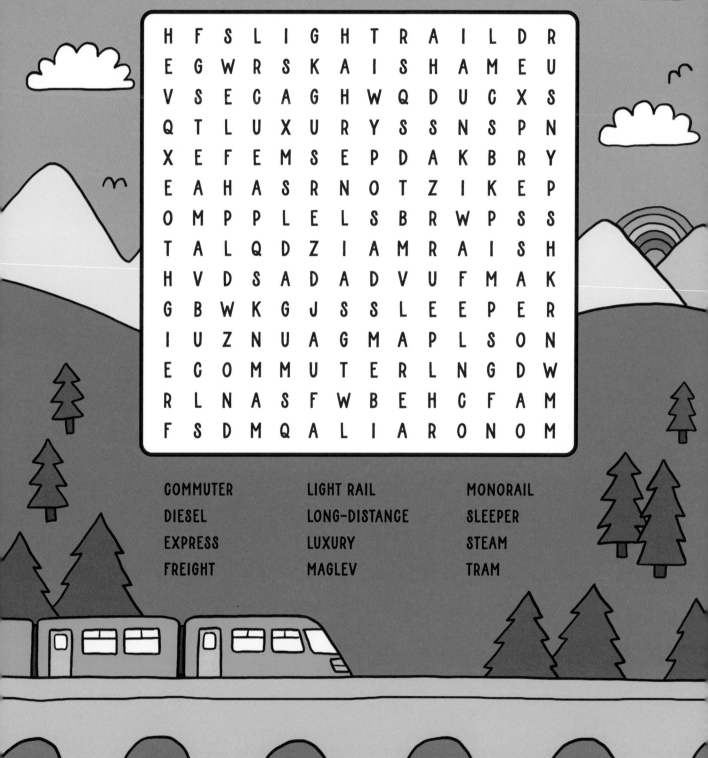

H	F	S	L	I	G	H	T	R	A	I	L	D	R
E	G	W	R	S	K	A	I	S	H	A	M	E	U
V	S	E	C	A	G	H	W	Q	D	U	C	X	S
Q	T	L	U	X	U	R	Y	S	S	N	S	P	N
X	E	F	E	M	S	E	P	D	A	K	B	R	Y
E	A	H	A	S	R	N	O	T	Z	I	K	E	P
O	M	P	P	L	E	L	S	B	R	W	P	S	S
T	A	L	Q	D	Z	I	A	M	R	A	I	S	H
H	V	D	S	A	D	A	D	V	U	F	M	A	K
G	B	W	K	G	J	S	S	L	E	E	P	E	R
I	U	Z	N	U	A	G	M	A	P	L	S	O	N
E	C	O	M	M	U	T	E	R	L	N	G	D	W
R	L	N	A	S	F	W	B	E	H	C	F	A	M
F	S	D	M	Q	A	L	I	A	R	O	N	O	M

COMMUTER

DIESEL

EXPRESS

FREIGHT

LIGHT RAIL

LONG-DISTANCE

LUXURY

MAGLEV

MONORAIL

SLEEPER

STEAM

TRAM

CLIMBING CODES

SOLVE THE PROBLEMS TO FIGURE OUT THE CODE.
THEN ANSWER THE QUESTION BELOW.

| A | 13 - 6 = ___ |

| C | 11 + 5 = ___ |

| I | 19 - 10 = ___ |

| K | 20 - 18 = ___ |

| L | 7 + 3 = ___ |

| O | 18 - 5 = ___ |

| R | 10 + 5 = ___ |

What is the name for trains that can climb mountains?

___ ___ ___   ___ ___   ___ ___ ___ ___   ___ ___ ___ ___ ___ ___ ___ ___
16 13 8   13 15   15 7 16 2   15 7 9 10 11 7 20 6

| W | 6 + 5 = ___ |

| Y | 18 + 2 = ___ |

| S | 10 - 4 = ___ |

| G | 17 - 9 = ___ |

BUSY STREET

YOUR TRAIN IS PASSING THROUGH A TOWN.
WHAT DO YOU SEE OUT THE WINDOW?
TURN THIS STREET INTO A BUSY SCENE.

SNAP-DOKU

FILL IN THE GRIDS SO THAT EACH ROW, COLUMN, AND SECTION CONTAINS ALL THE LETTERS OF THE WORD BELOW EACH GRID.

The Shanghai Metro in China is the longest metro system in the world.

CARS

TREE

COWS

PERFECT POSTER

DESIGN A POSTER FOR YOUR FAVORITE PLACE TO GO BY TRAIN.
WHAT'S YOUR FAVORITE THING TO DO OR SEE THERE? DRAW IT HERE.

I SPY

CAN YOU SPOT ALL THESE THINGS OUT THE TRAIN WINDOW? CHECK OFF EACH ONE AS YOU FIND THEM.

- [ ] BLACKBIRD
- [ ] RABBIT
- [ ] GREY CAT
- [ ] TWO COWS
- [ ] FLOWERPOT
- [ ] FISH

- [ ] ANCHOR
- [ ] FISHING ROD
- [ ] YELLOW HAT
- [ ] LIFEBUOY
- [ ] GREEN DOOR
- [ ] THREE LAMP POSTS

TIME TO TRAVEL

SOLVE THE CLUES AND FILL IN THE CROSSWORD.

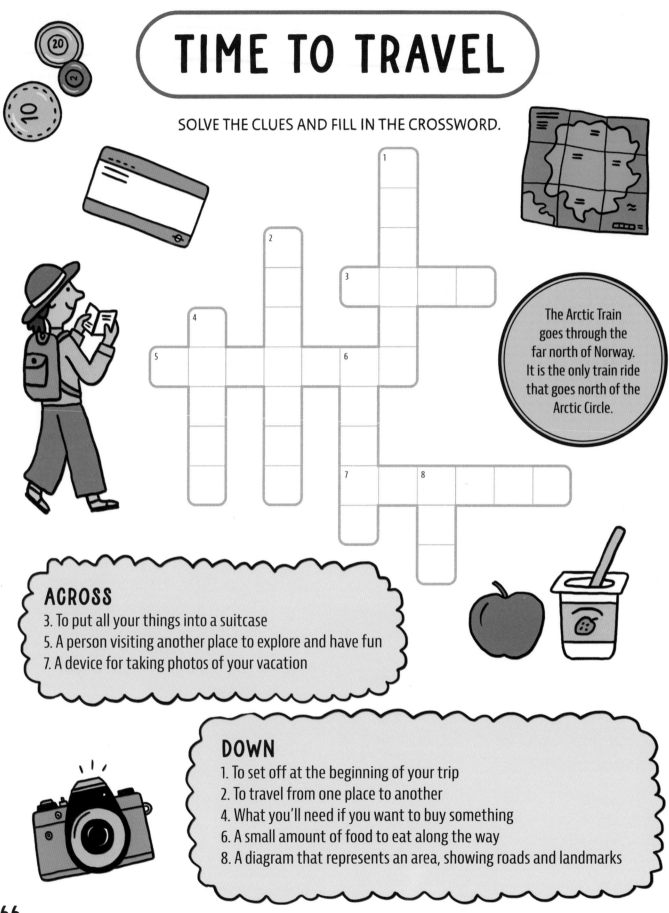

The Arctic Train goes through the far north of Norway. It is the only train ride that goes north of the Arctic Circle.

ACROSS
3. To put all your things into a suitcase
5. A person visiting another place to explore and have fun
7. A device for taking photos of your vacation

DOWN
1. To set off at the beginning of your trip
2. To travel from one place to another
4. What you'll need if you want to buy something
6. A small amount of food to eat along the way
8. A diagram that represents an area, showing roads and landmarks

TRAVEL FUNNIES

DRAW LINES TO MATCH EACH JOKE
TO ITS PUNCHLINE.

It is thought that soldiers known as the Knights Templar were the first to use luggage with wheels more than 800 years ago.

1 What travels up and down hills, through cities and towns, over bridges, and through tunnels, but never moves?

A A stamp!

2 What travels all around the world but stays in one corner?

B Ohio!

3 Which U.S. state is round at the ends and high in the middle?

C To the Baaa-hamas!

4 How do bees like to travel?

D A road!

5 Where did the sheep go on vacation?

E They take the buzz!

LOVE TO TRAVEL

WRITE AN ACROSTIC POEM ABOUT HOW TRAVELING MAKES YOU FEEL AND WHY YOU LIKE IT. USE THE LETTERS OF THE WORD "TRAVEL" BELOW TO START EACH LINE.

T _____

R _____

A _____

V _____

E _____

L _____

Of all the countries in the world, France is the one travelers visit most.

LOST LUGGAGE

FOLLOW THE LINES TO HELP EACH PASSENGER FIND THEIR MISSING LUGGAGE.

A luggage tracker is a small electronic device that connects to a mobile phone. It tracks the location of the bag it is attached to.

PASSENGER PERSPECTIVE

FOLLOW THESE STEPS TO DRAW A PASSENGER TRAIN. USE PERSPECTIVE TO MAKE IT LOOK LIKE IT'S COMING TOWARD YOU!

1

On the left side of your page, draw three lines down and three lines across to make a 2x2 grid.

2

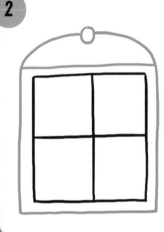

Draw a square around the outside of the grid, then draw a curved line over the top of the square. Add a circle in the center of the curved line.

3

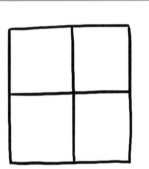

Below your grid, draw a slanted rectangle shape with a notch in it, as shown. In the grid, draw two small squares and two small circles—these will be the lights— plus two windows above them.

4

Draw a dot on the right side of your page to help add perspective. From the small circle, draw a straight line connecting to the dot.

5

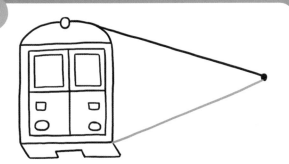

From the bottom-right corner of the large square, draw another straight line connecting to the dot on the right.

6

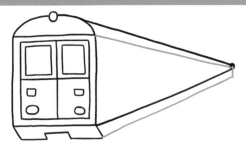

Draw a short line straight down from the dot. Join it to the bottom-right corner of the slanted rectangle with a line, then draw another line to join the dot to the top-right corner of the square.

7

Draw lines to divide your train into railcars. Shade in the bottom of the slanted rectangle, as shown, and add two lines below it for tracks.

8

Add grid lines to the slanted rectangle shape, as shown. Draw windows on the railcars, along with any other details you'd like to include.

9

Now color your train!

GRIDLOCK

THE TRAIN IS STUCK AT A RED SIGNAL! FIT THESE THINGS
YOU MIGHT SEE OUT THE WINDOW INTO THE GRID.

4 LETTERS
BIRD
SIGN

5 LETTERS
TRACK
WIRES

6 LETTERS
SIGNAL
POINTS

8 LETTERS
CROSSING

Melbourne,
Australia is home
to the largest
tram network
of any city.

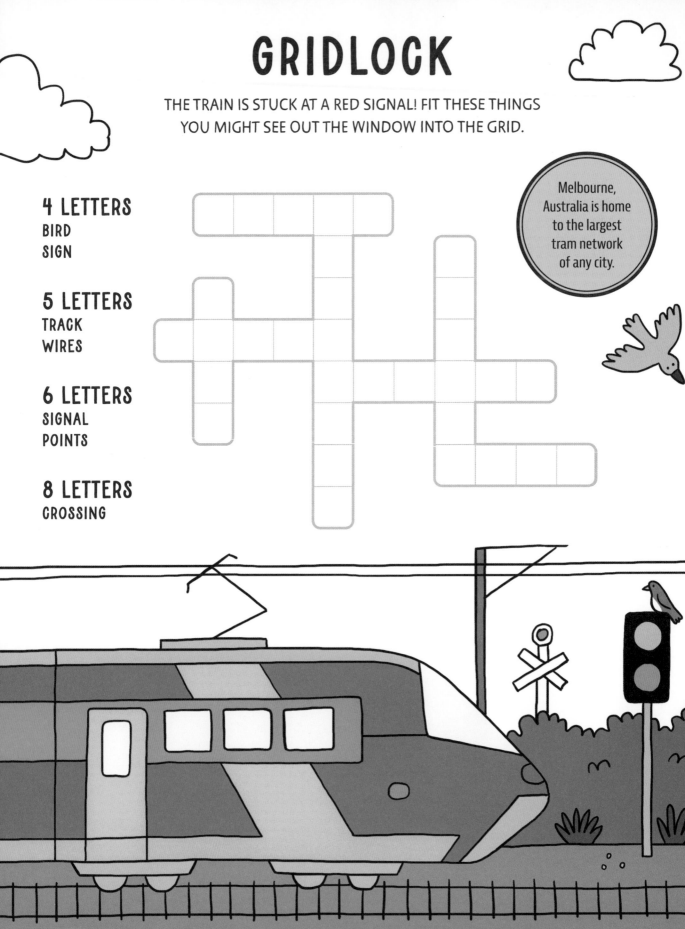

PACKED TO THE BRIM

LOOK CLOSELY AT THIS PICTURE OF A SUITCASE.
WHAT CAN YOU SPOT INSIDE? TRY TO REMEMBER AS MANY DETAILS
AS YOU CAN, THEN TURN THE PAGE TO TEST YOUR MEMORY.

PACKED TO THE BRIM

THINK BACK TO THE PICTURE OF THE OPEN SUITCASE ON THE PREVIOUS PAGE. CAN YOU ANSWER ALL THESE QUESTIONS?

1
What color were the gloves?

_____

2
What was packed in the top-left corner of the suitcase?

_____

3
What was on top of the diary?

_____

4
How many teddy bears were there?

_____

5
What color was the hair dryer?

_____

6
What color was the flask?

_____

7
Did the passenger remember their toothbrush?

_____

RIDDLE ME THIS

GET YOUR BRAIN IN GEAR TO SOLVE THESE
TRICKY TRAVEL QUESTIONS.

1
There are four
trains on the tracks. Train A
is longer than train B, but
shorter than train C. Train D is
the longest train. Which is the
shortest train?

_____

2
I travel from there to
here by disappearing,
and from here to there by
reappearing. What am I?

_____

SUDOKU CHALLENGE

FILL IN THE GRID SO THAT EACH ROW, COLUMN, AND SECTION
CONTAINS ALL THE LETTERS OF THE WORD "TRACKS."

T		A		C	K	S
		K		A		R
R				K	C	
C	K				S	A
		R			A	C
		C		T		

Some long-distance
trains have observation
cars. They are often at the
end of the train and have
large windows, which
allow riders to take
in the sights.

75

CONNECT THE DOTS TO REVEAL A SUPER-LONG
PASSENGER TRAIN. THEN COLOR THE PICTURE.

TO THE FUTURE

CAN YOU FIND ALL THE WORDS IN THE GRID?

```
F W Z J I F K O S S Z T U P
C L I M A T E M D X S H J L
I Q E H T X O T Y A O P G V
T A C B P O I Y F G K H I C
E N U I T D C V B N E M I B
N F X H V U O M O D E R N E
G Z F P I O N E H D L M V L
A Q C I U G D R G H S L E E
M V T S C P H A I C M B N C
X E W V C I Y S N E H C T T
C T H Q U I E T P R F M I R
B R Z H N M X N O E D E V I
I H T E S P Y L T R E M E C
D F U T U R I S T I C D X B
```

CLIMATE	FUTURISTIC	MODERN
ELECTRIC	HIGH-SPEED	QUIET
EFFICIENT	INVENTIVE	SLEEK
FAST	MAGNETIC	SMOOTH

Some cities around the world have autonomous trains, which are trains that drive themselves!

RUSH HOUR

LOOK CLOSELY AT THIS BUSY STATION.
THEN ANSWER THE QUESTIONS BELOW.

Japan's Shinjuku Station in Tokyo is the world's busiest station. More than 3.6 million people use it each day.

1. How many people can you count? _____

2. What time does the clock show? _____

3. How many people are wearing glasses? _____

4. How many dogs are there? _____

5. How many birds do you see? _____

6. What color is the balloon? _____

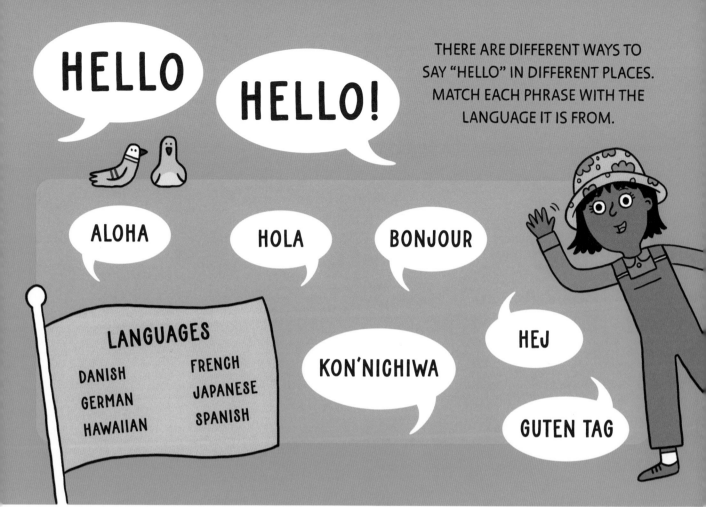

HELLO

HELLO!

THERE ARE DIFFERENT WAYS TO SAY "HELLO" IN DIFFERENT PLACES. MATCH EACH PHRASE WITH THE LANGUAGE IT IS FROM.

ALOHA

HOLA

BONJOUR

HEJ

KON'NICHIWA

GUTEN TAG

LANGUAGES

DANISH
GERMAN
HAWAIIAN
FRENCH
JAPANESE
SPANISH

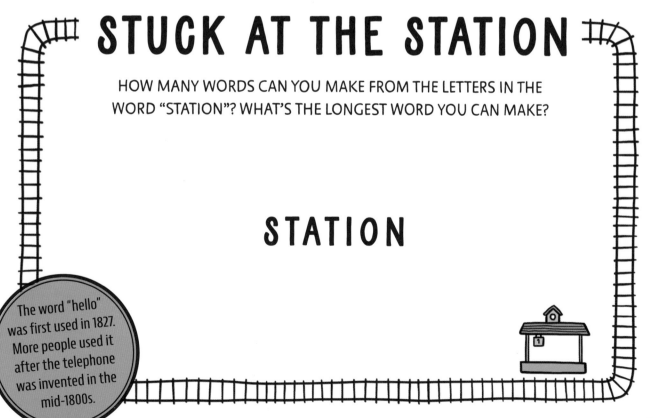

STUCK AT THE STATION

HOW MANY WORDS CAN YOU MAKE FROM THE LETTERS IN THE WORD "STATION"? WHAT'S THE LONGEST WORD YOU CAN MAKE?

STATION

The word "hello" was first used in 1827. More people used it after the telephone was invented in the mid-1800s.

STAYING ON TRACK

WHICH TRACK GETS THE TRAIN FROM STATION 1 TO STATION 2?

The Trans-Siberian Railroad in Russia is the longest train route in the world. It takes six days to make the whole journey!

MADE YOU LAUGH

DRAW LINES TO MATCH EACH JOKE
TO ITS PUNCHLINE.

Some train cars are large enough to carry road vehicles. The vehicles are locked in place so they do not move.

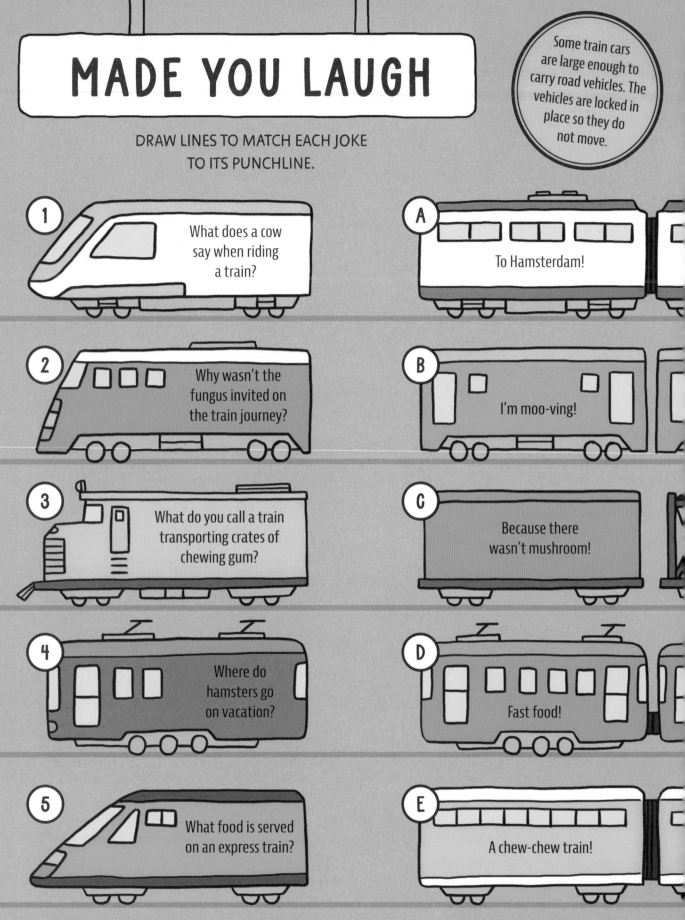

1 What does a cow say when riding a train?

A To Hamsterdam!

2 Why wasn't the fungus invited on the train journey?

B I'm moo-ving!

3 What do you call a train transporting crates of chewing gum?

C Because there wasn't mushroom!

4 Where do hamsters go on vacation?

D Fast food!

5 What food is served on an express train?

E A chew-chew train!

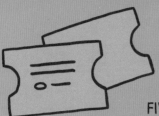

FAMILY FUN

FIVE FAMILIES ARE GOING TO FIVE DIFFERENT PLACES.
USE THE CLUES TO FIGURE OUT WHICH FAMILY IS GOING WHERE.

	JONESES	TAYLORS	SANDOVALS	PATELS	CHENS
MOUNTAINS					
FOREST					
BEACH					
CITY					
FARM					

Mark each place they are not going with an "X." Put a check mark for the place each family is going.

CLUES

1. The Joneses don't like nature vacations.
3. The Sandovals live too far from the mountains, and they're not fond of farms.
4. The youngest Patel is allergic to farm animals.
5. The Taylors enjoy time spent with animals such as horses, cows, and pigs.
2. The Chens have packed towels and sunscreen. They are looking forward to swimming in the sea.

WHOSE SHADOW?

WHICH PASSENGER DOES THIS SHADOW BELONG TO?

COUNTRY SEARCH

CAN YOU FIND ALL THE WORDS IN THE GRID?

```
Y C M N V T H A I L A N D P
S A F E G H J K L N E P A L
M N V C G B F D A H J K R E
R A L U M Y Y I H T C V I L
T D H G F E P D J U A H N A
L A F Q K W E T R I U I D N
K T Y R H G S X L D F H I A
M I U G S B R A Z I L D A W
E T U M A S R D A F G H K S
X T R E W T Q A Z N X C V T
I J S D S F U K R A I N E O
C Y K U T Y S D V C B H N B
O Y A W R O N V B N M E C I
U T B K I N D O N E S I A L
```

AUSTRALIA EGYPT NEPAL
BOTSWANA FIJI NORWAY
BRAZIL INDIA THAILAND
CANADA INDONESIA TURKEY
CHINA MEXICO UKRAINE

North America's longest train journey connects the Canadian cities of Toronto in the east and Vancouver in the west. The trip takes four days!

PEOPLE WATCHING

WHO IS RIDING THIS TRAIN? IT'S UP TO YOU!
DOODLE FACES ON THE PASSENGERS.

To celebrate 175 years of railroads in Switzerland, a 100-railcar train was introduced. It ran for just one day, but broke the record for the world's longest passenger train.

RECORD-BREAKERS

DRAW LINES TO MATCH EACH ROSETTE TO THE TROPHY
SHOWING THE WORLD RECORD IT BROKE.

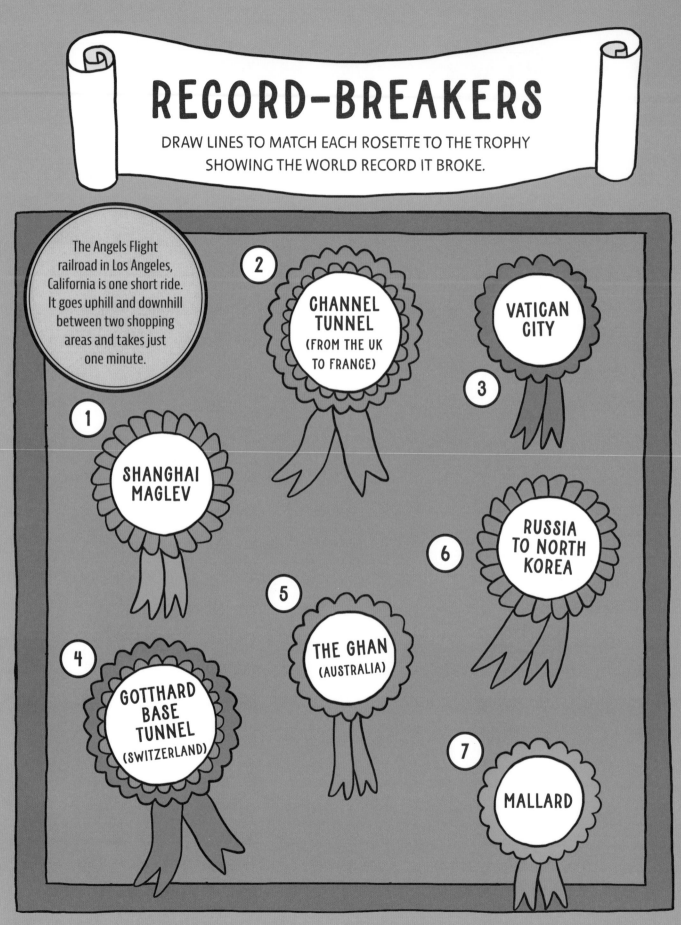

The Angels Flight railroad in Los Angeles, California is one short ride. It goes uphill and downhill between two shopping areas and takes just one minute.

2 — CHANNEL TUNNEL (FROM THE UK TO FRANCE)

3 — VATICAN CITY

1 — SHANGHAI MAGLEV

6 — RUSSIA TO NORTH KOREA

5 — THE GHAN (AUSTRALIA)

4 — GOTTHARD BASE TUNNEL (SWITZERLAND)

7 — MALLARD

FOREST FINDS

- [ ] OWL
- [ ] FROG
- [ ] WHITE SHOES
- [ ] FOX
- [ ] BUTTERFLY
- [ ] SIGNPOST

CAN YOU SPOT ALL THE ITEMS LISTED BELOW THROUGH THE TRAIN WINDOW? CHECK OFF EACH ONE AS YOU FIND THEM.

A ride on the Grand Canyon Railway in Arizona, USA, provides views of forests and prairies, wild animals, and the Grand Canyon itself.

- [ ] RED HELMET
- [ ] YELLOW BIKE
- [ ] LOG PILE
- [ ] WHITE FLOWER
- [ ] FOUR TOADSTOOLS
- [ ] THREE WHITE BIRDS

SIGHTSEEING SCRAMBLE

UNSCRAMBLE THE WORDS TO UNCOVER FAMOUS LANDMARKS THAT YOU CAN VISIT BY TRAIN. USE THE CLUES ABOVE THE PICTURES TO HELP YOU.

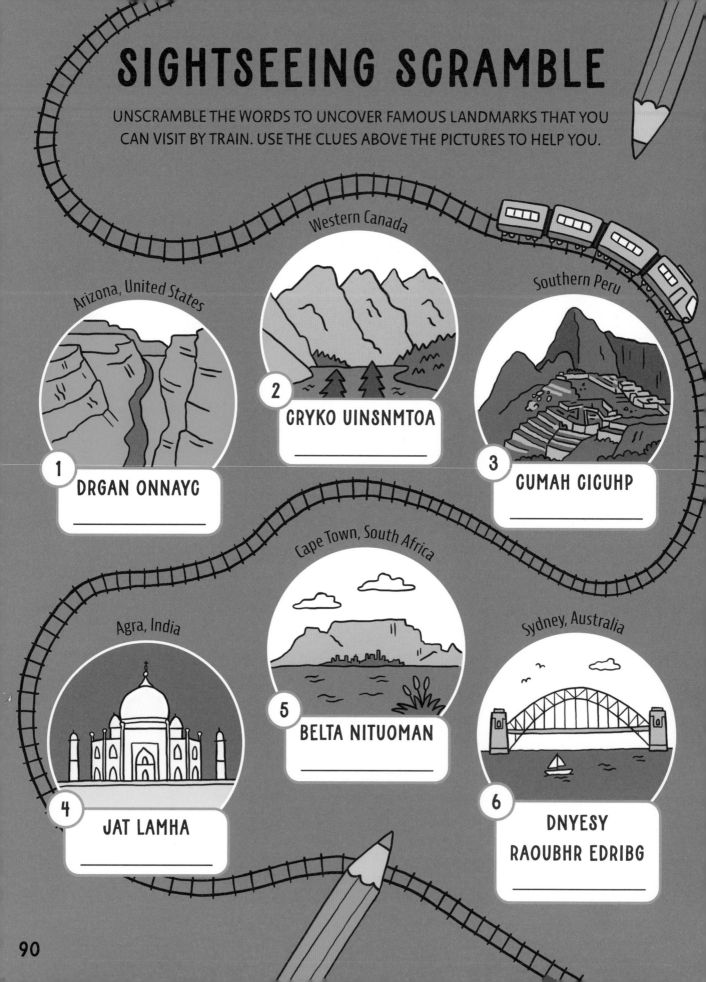

Western Canada

2 GRYKO UINSNMTOA
_____

Arizona, United States

1 DRGAN ONNAYC
_____

Southern Peru

3 CUMAH CICUHP
_____

Agra, India

4 JAT LAMHA
_____

Cape Town, South Africa

5 BELTA NITUOMAN
_____

Sydney, Australia

6 DNYESY RAOUBHR EDRIBG
_____

FULL STEAM AHEAD

The Hogwarts Express train from the Harry Potter movies was modeled after Scotland's Jacobite steam train.

FIND AND CIRCLE THE 10 DIFFERENCES BETWEEN THESE TWO PICTURES.

454

454

LOST LETTERS

THESE COUNTRIES ARE MISSING SOME OF
THEIR LETTERS. CAN YOU FILL IN THE BLANKS
USING THE MISSING LETTERS BELOW?

The symbols on
a flag usually represent a
part of a country's history or
culture. Colors often represent
parts of nature.
For example, the color
blue for the sea.

1. IN _ _ A

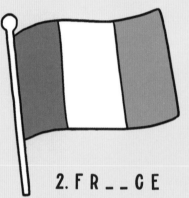

2. FR _ _ CE

3. AL _ _ RIA

4. COL _ _ BIA

5. NEW
Z _ _ LAND

6. ME _ _ CO

EA   AN   GE   OM   DI   XI

CODE OF CONDUCT

HOW MANY WORDS CAN YOU MAKE FROM THE LETTERS IN THE WORD "CONDUCTOR"? WHAT IS THE LONGEST WORD YOU CAN MAKE?

CONDUCTOR

In 1934, a train known as The Flying Scotsman, which ran between Scotland and England, became the first steam train to reach speeds of 100 miles per hour (161 kph).

SUDOKU CHALLENGE

FILL IN THE GRID SO THAT EACH ROW, COLUMN, AND SECTION CONTAINS ALL THE LETTERS OF THE WORD "ENGINE."

E	N	G	I		E
N	I				E
		E	N		
N	E	N		I	G
G	E		E		N
	N		G	E	I

ANSWERS

p2

p3  = 3   = 6   = 5

p4 1. SYDNEY, 2. ISTANBUL,
3. SHANGHAI, 4. LONDON,
5. TORONTO, 6. CHICAGO

p5

P	A	C	K
C	K	P	A
A	P	K	C
K	C	A	P

p6

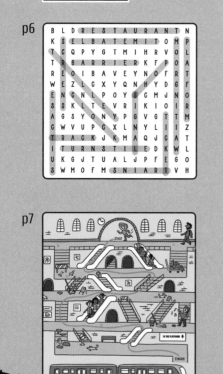

p7

p8-9

The ticket from Auckland to Wellington is one-way only.

p13 AUSTRALIA

p14-15

p16

L	I	R	A
R	A	L	I
I	R	A	L
A	L	I	R

p17 DON BELAYTE

p18

YEN, EURO, RUPEE, RAND, REAL, DOLLAR, POUND, FRANC

p19

STATION, TUNNEL, TICKET, CROSSING, ENGINE, GOAL, ALTER, TRACK, EXPRESS

p20-21

1. Prague, 2. Paris,
3. Yes, they will make it, 4. Nice,
5. 5B, 6. No, they didn't make it,
7. Platform 2, 8. 18 minutes

p22 1. MONORAIL, 2. EXPRESS,
3. MAGLEV, 4. TRAM, 5. FREIGHT

p25

p26

p27 WISH YOU WERE HERE

p28

CLOTHES, TOOTHBRUSH, HAIRBRUSH, HEADPHONES, TOOTHPASTE, SNACKS, TICKET, PYJAMAS, SOCKS, PILLOW, BOOKS

p29 1-E, 2-C, 3-D, 4-A, 5-B

p30-31

p32 1. Rocket, 2. Mallard, 3. Métro,
4. "Big Boy," 5. Bullet Trains

p33 1. Three carriages
2. Whatever color your hair is. You're the driver!
3. One enters at 8am and the other at 8pm

p40

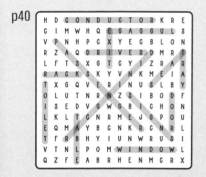

p42 1. Red, 2. Enjoy your journey!,
3. Ice cream, 4. Two, 5. Blue,
6. Eleven

p47 WELCOME TO TRAIN TOWN

p51

p53 1. BRAKES, 2. CAB, 3. WHEELS,
4. DOOR, 5. WINDSHIELD,
6. HEADLIGHTS

p54 1. BEACH, 2. CITY,
3. MUSEUM, 4. PLAYGROUND,
5. MOUNTAIN, 6. COUNTRYSIDE,
7. CASTLE, 8. THEATER

p55

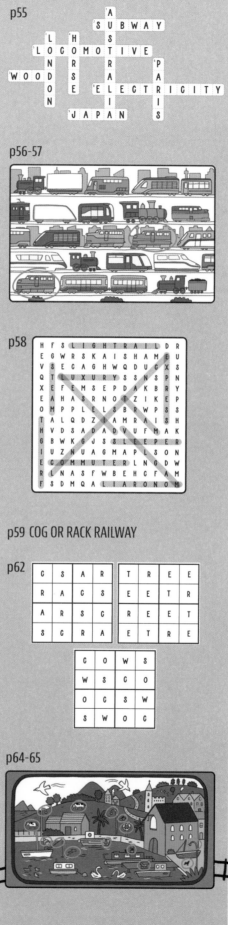

p56-57

p58

p59 COG OR RACK RAILWAY

p62

C	S	A	R
R	A	C	S
A	R	S	C
S	S	C	R	A

T	R	E	E
S	E	E	T	R
S	C	R	E	E	T
E	T	R	E

C	O	W	S
W	S	C	O
O	C	S	W
S	W	O	C

p64-65

p66

p67 1-D, 2-A, 3-B, 4-E, 5-C

p69 1-B, 2-D, 3-A, 4-C

p72

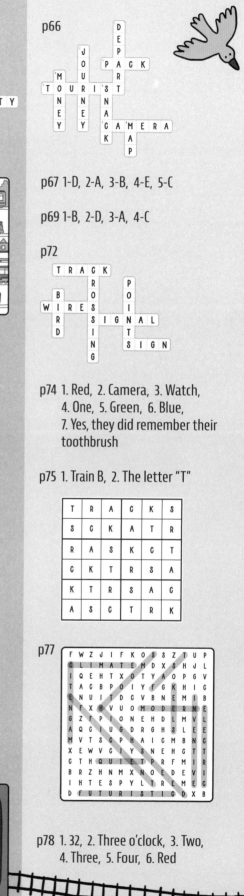

p74 1. Red, 2. Camera, 3. Watch,
4. One, 5. Green, 6. Blue,
7. Yes, they did remember their toothbrush

p75 1. Train B, 2. The letter "T"

T	R	A	C	K	S
S	C	K	A	T	R
R	A	S	K	C	T
C	K	T	R	S	A
K	T	R	S	A	C
A	S	C	T	R	K

p77

p78 1. 32, 2. Three o'clock, 3. Two,
4. Three, 5. Four, 6. Red

95

p79 Aloha – Hawaiian
Hola – Spanish
Bonjour – French
Kon'nichiwa – Japanese
Hej – Danish
Guten Tag – German

p80-81
Track 2

p82 1-B, 2-C, 3-E, 4-A, 5-D

p83 Joneses – City
Taylors – Farm
Sandovals – Forest
Patels – Mountains
Chens – Beach

WHOSE SHADOW?
The shadow belongs to
passenger 2

p84
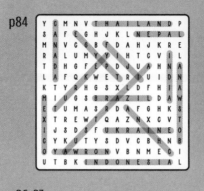

p86-87
1-E, 2-F, 3-D, 4-C, 5-B, 6-A, 7-G

p88-89

p90 1. GRAND CANYON, 2. ROCKY
MOUNTAINS, 3. MACHU PICCHU,
4. TAJ MAHAL, 5. TABLE MOUNTAIN,
6. SYDNEY HARBOUR BRIDGE

p91

p92 1. INDIA, 2. FRANCE, 3. ALGERIA,
4. COLOMBIA, 5. NEW ZEALAND,
6. MEXICO

p.93

E	N	G	I	N	E
N	I	E	N	G	E
I	G	E	N	E	N
N	E	N	E	I	G
G	E	I	E	N	N
E	N	N	G	E	I

ACKNOWLEDGEMENTS

Commissioned and project managed by Duck Egg Blue Limited

Author: Laura Baker
Editor: Priyanka Lamichhane
Illustrator: Sophie Foster
Designers: Andy Mansfield, Stephen Scanlan and
Duck Egg Blue Limited
Publishing Director: Piers Pickard
Publisher: Rebecca Hunt
Art Director: Andy Mansfield
Print Production: Nigel Longuet

Published in May 2024 by Lonely Planet Global Limited
CRN: 554153
ISBN: 978 1 83758 298 3
www.lonelyplanet.com/kids
© Lonely Planet 2024

10 9 8 7 6 5 4 3 2 1

Printed in China

STAY IN TOUCH

lonelyplanet.com/contact

Lonely Planet Office:
IRELAND
Digital Depot, Roe Lane
(off Thomas St), Digital Hub,
Dublin 8, D08 TCV4, Ireland

MIX
Paper from
responsible sources
FSC™ C021741

Paper in this book is certified against the
Forest Stewardship Council™ standards.
FSC™ promotes environmentally responsible,
socially beneficial and economically viable
management of the world's forests.